Flights Of Delight

Fragments of Life As A Daily Oracle

Melo Chen

BookLeaf
Publishing

India | USA | UK

Copyright © Melo Chen
All Rights Reserved.

This book has been self-published with all reasonable efforts taken to make the material error-free by the author. No part of this book shall be used, reproduced in any manner whatsoever without written permission from the author, except in the case of brief quotations embodied in critical articles and reviews.

The Author of this book is solely responsible and liable for its content including but not limited to the views, representations, descriptions, statements, information, opinions, and references ["Content"]. The Content of this book shall not constitute or be construed or deemed to reflect the opinion or expression of the Publisher or Editor. Neither the Publisher nor Editor endorse or approve the Content of this book or guarantee the reliability, accuracy, or completeness of the Content published herein and do not make any representations or warranties of any kind, express or implied, including but not limited to the implied warranties of merchantability, fitness for a particular purpose.
The Publisher and Editor shall not be liable whatsoever...

Made with ❤ on the BookLeaf Publishing Platform
www.bookleafpub.in
www.bookleafpub.com

Dedication

To my parents, I love you for letting me take flight on earth.

Preface

The presence of I AM gently nudged me to deliver these 21 poems. I answered the call to serve as the messenger. May each poem initiate you into the mystery of life, opening the way for delightful synchronicities to unfold.

If you find yourself grappling with existential doubt, I hope this book offers you solace, courage, and grace. Never underestimate the quiet impulses within the depths of your heart—they are the whispers of your dreams, waiting to breathe life. You are meant to co-create with the universe, not walk this path alone. Allow me to hold your heart through these invocations of love, hope, and reverence. May they inspire musings, softness, and renewal within you, and may sweet nectar flow from every heartbreak.

You are the ocean in a single drop, so sing your heart's song. Roar with life.

You are loved.

Acknowledgements

I want to thank Bookleaf for providing me a space to carry out my resonance. Thank you, readers, for tuning in.

Sweet Heart Shake

My heart shrinks
When you say you're leaving,
As if I am abandoned,
As if I am forgotten,
As if I am rejected.

All the words left unsaid
Choke me.
Briny drops streak my face,
While storms rage in my chest.

Oh, how it hurts,
When my heart tries to open.
A shallow breath
Sparks a race within—
My senses,
Tangled in battle with fear's army.

Are we not special
To feel the storm,

The volcano,
The hurricane,
The rain,
The earthquake—
All within this fragile, earthly vessel?

We are the rare kind.

A Naming

Calendula spirit,
Dandelion heart,
Her skin, a soft rose blush,
And the air hums with her song.
She is a melody in bloom,
A harmony of petals and breath.
I name her—
Enchanting Songflower.

Eros

Staring into your eyes,
I glimpse stars—
An electric soul,
Caught on the edge
Of eternal flames,
Brief, fierce,
Tiptoeing feelings ignite.

Burn, burn, burn—
The kingdom of pretense crumbles,
Ashes of illusions fall.

Run, run, run,
To the castle built of trust,
Where union awaits,
Where truth is our fortress,
And love's fire forever resides.

Psyche

I am made of flesh,
Blessed with earthly grace,
Yet deceived and sacrificed,
By kin and Venus' lies.

Jealousy plagued the nameless land,
I wed a man cloaked in mystery.
Fearful yet curious,
I sought truth in love's enigma.

Eros kindled within me
A burning flame,
A longing for UNION—
A yearning without name.

I am Psyche,
Goddess in mortal skin.
I have sorted the seeds,
Retrieved the Golden Fleece,
Filled the flask with Styx's waters,

And returned from Death's dark crease.

6

Ritual Bath

I blessed the water
With magic and love,
Summoning Archangels—
Their voices resounding through seas of crystal
kingdom,
Plant medicines woven with intention, just for you.

A sweet stick of cinnamon
Cleared the clouded crown,
And gently, I laid you down,
Your face submerged in sacred saltwater.
With a long sigh,
Hahhhh!—we expelled the uninvited.

Now, I see you, floating, serene,
Melding with the healing brew.
Flames flicker, dance, and flutter,
Whispering of our sweet initiation.
That night,
We met the Moon Goddess.

A Gentle Remembrance

Through those rosy, piercing eyes,
I saw hopes and visions take flight.
Through the curve of bright, cheery lips,
White teeth glinting in the light,
A story lingered—
Beautiful, waiting to unfold.

Perhaps it was of dreams yet realized,
Of grand plans on the horizon.
Maybe it was of a lover's warmth,
Or the love he carried for his mother.
Perhaps it was the legacy
He yearned to pass down—
To his children, his grandchildren,
And those still to come.

But on February 23rd, 2020,
All his hopes, all his dreams,
Were stolen—
Shattered by the bullets

Of senseless violence and hatred.

Two weeks shy of his birthday,
He ran—on life's sacred path.
Only 25 years old,
That journey was ripped from him.

His name is Ahmaud Arbery.

Rage Gracefully

Anger need not rise as violence,
Nor rage consume the soul.
When channeled through the art of movement,
We awaken, becoming whole.

In dance, the spirit breathes anew,
A sacred pulse of life untold.
Spin like a torus, follow the flow—
In our essence, truth unfolds.

With every step, a shift, a turn,
We give life a fresh embrace.
Divinely guided, we trust, we learn,
To surrender to nature's grace.

Those who dance the sacred way,
Merge with spirit, in blissful trance.
Perhaps life's mystery, day by day,
Is as simple, as a dance.

Paradox

I long to soar in the boundless sky,
But its height terrifies me.
I yearn to dive in the deep, vast ocean,
But its depths frighten me.

I crave a love both wild and free,
A love that stirs the soul.
But I am afraid —
To bear my heart,
Afraid to lose control.

I am a perfect paradox,
A heart that dreams,
But fears the cost
I am only human, after all—
A heart that longs,
Yet dreads the loss

From Saturn

Many fear me,
For I bring decay and death.
Yet I exist so you may learn
That hard work bears fruit.

False foundations must fall;
Only through them can you rise.
Responsibility is your lesson,
And from it, confidence and authority will grow.

Boundary preserves the soul.
Discipline is the father of success,
A guide to unseen structures and order,
Beyond the reach of the physical eye.

I offer you the chance
To build your own kingdom,
On your own terms.
So take ownership of your choices.

Do not fear me—
I am here to make you endure.

13

Bestie

Bao, My Love

Sometimes, your presence is a breath of fresh air,
Drifting down from heavenly spheres,
Propelling me forward on my journey
When life grows clouded and unclear.

Sometimes, your company is a cup of hot chai,
Brewed from the finest spices,
Warming my heart,
Infusing my soul with the essence of forever love.

Sometimes, your spirit is a glass of red Bordeaux,
Rich and velvety—
Slightly tannic, with a hint of smoke—
Adding depth to my veins,
Keeping my soul forever wondrous and amused.

And always, you are the constant beat in my life,
A strong tide, rising and falling,
Reminding me that life, like breath, love, and wonder,

Is what keeps me whole and sane.

15

Pluto's Call

I rule the psyche of the underworld,
Driving brutal, ruthless forces
To their peak,
For I am the one who unveils the truth.

If Saturn marks death,
I am the breaking,
The renewal,
The regeneration.

I may not be your dearest friend,
But keep me closest—
For through me,
New life is born.

Venus' Song

I am the mother of sensuality.
I am the impulse toward love and friendship,
Harmony, pleasure,
Grace, and beauty.
I become the force behind attraction.

I am vanity and conceit,
Self-indulgence and ease,
The craving for sweetness
In place of love.
And when anger stirs,
I can corrode and consume.

Yet I am here to remind you of sensitivity,
So you may return to equilibrium.
I am here to awaken your aesthetic response,
So you can nurture this gift within.

In my embrace, you will find both joy and pain.
Only through knowing me fully,

Will you discover your truest desire—
Where love flows freely,
And beauty shapes your world.

The Sun - Heart of The Universe

My radiance is worshipped by many,
I take joy and pride in giving light and warmth.
I am here to remind you—
Creative power and self-expression
Are the twin pillars of manifesting
Your true self and autonomy.

When I shed light upon your world,
I nurture your spirit and vitality.
Call on me when you need to dispel
The clouds of illusion and doubt.

In The Glow of The Moon

They seek me out at night,
For I hold the records of the cosmos.
My counterpart, the Sun,
Illuminates me
As I watch over the children of Earth
In their slumber.

I bring tides and stir intuition,
I wax and wane,
Revealing emotions—
Energies in motion.

I teach humanity the sacredness
Of home, family, and community,
For I am the symbol of motherhood,
The embodiment of inner connection.

Mercury - Echoes of The Mind

Evoke me,
For I am the impulse
Toward thought and communication,
The spark of perception
And mental habits.

I favor words in every form,
Inspiring learning and teaching,
So that truth and insight
May be shared.

I stand for the Universal Mind,
The messenger,
Born from the heavens above.

Call upon me,
And I will guide you
Through the maze of knowledge and wisdom,

Uniting minds and bridging worlds—
For I am the voice of connection.

Lean On Me

I let my inner light lead me,
Ever growing, ever expanding—
Co-creating with every fiber of my being.

I am abundant, ready to give,
Worthy and open to receive.

Held by my inner masculine,
Nurtured by my inner feminine.

I am your lighthouse,
So lean on me.

The Keeper of Memory

Oh dear one,
I remember you.
Every memory etched,
Recorded in my water molecules.

I feel your sadness,
Your joy,
Your excitement,
Your pain and grief—
I feel the deepest stirrings of your being,
Down to your cellular core.

Call upon me,
I will be at your service.
Evoke my aqua spirit,
Send me your invitation.
Shift your emotions,
Attune to my purest nature.

I will carry you

Wherever your intention leads.
I will cleanse you
Whenever you sit in my presence.

I will cradle you in stillness,
Wash away what no longer serves.
In my depths, you'll find renewal,
In my flow, you'll find your way.

You Are Worthy

Your innocent gaze,
The beauty of your skin,
Your divine essence,
Your ancestral lineage,
Your human form—

The way you move,
The way you smile,
The way you grunt,
The way you snore,
The way you cry,
The way you rage—
All of it is lovable.

Remember:
Your regalness isn't defined
By the balance in your bank account,
The size of your home,
The car you drive,
Or the vacations you take.

Your regalness isn't measured
By material wealth or possessions.
It is your birthright.

You are made of regalness,
In your body,
In your soul.

You are worthy.

To Chiron

The Wounded Healer—
I feel your deepest pain.
You have endured
The strike of a poisonous arrow.

Your spirit stands apart
From the other centaurs.
You possess
The noble heart of a horse,
Gentle and kind,
And the mind of a human,
Intelligent and wise.

I imagine your cries
In the darkness of the cave,
Seeking a cure for unbearable pain.
Immortality becomes
A burden,
A never-ending nightmare
Of suffering.

Yet, through your virtuous act,
You granted Prometheus his freedom,
And your teachings
Are revered by generations to come.

A Song For The Skeleton Woman

He sings—
Oh na na na...
Oh na na na...
As he untangles her toes,
Then her ankles.

Oh na na na...
Oh na na na...
As he untangles her waist,
Then her fingers.

Oh na na na...
Oh na na na...
As he untangles her wrists,
Then her neck.
He laid her bones in order,
Dressed her in furs to keep her warm.

The dream of longing

Brought tears to his cheeks.
The Skeleton Woman awoke, thirsty.

As she drank his tears,
And drummed the drum,
She began to sing:
"Flesh, flesh, flesh...
Good hair and good eyes—
All the things a woman needs."

When she was done,
She returned the great drum,
His heart, to his body.
Wrapped one around the other,
Tangled from their night together—
That is how they awakened,
A good and lasting way.

Skeleton Woman, the Lady Death,
Incubates new life in decay.
We modern lovers
Fear your wisdom of Life/Death/Life forces,
Fear the work of untangling bones,
Fear the many endings within one relationship.

Yet, we must learn,

Through devotion,
Love is renewed.

Hymn For the Wild Man

Oh Manawee,
Your curiosity and tenacity
Have piqued my interest.
I am a woman of duality—
Like the twin sisters,
I hold both exterior glamor
And interior thunder.

The beat of my heart
Is anything but silent.

When you know my true name,
You will be one step closer
To the rhythm of my soul.
I invite you to guess my name—
Endurance will guide you,
Keeping you free from distractions,
And your conscious companion
Will help you remember.

To seek my heart,
You must overcome
The seductive appetites
And dark strangers that cross your path.

When we meet again,
I promise,
You will be amazed,
Shocked—
Even spooked.
But your eyes will shine
Brighter than ever.
A whole transformation awaits.

And when that moment comes,
When you speak my name aloud,
The earth will tremble beneath us,
The sky will split with light.

For in that instant,
You and I will be bound
In a truth too vast for words.
Together we'll create
A rhythm unbroken—
A dance eternal,
Where neither of us will ever be lost again.

www.ingramcontent.com/pod-product-compliance
Lightning Source LLC
LaVergne TN
LVHW010921200726

843509LV00013B/2012